IMPRESSIONS of

BRITAIN'S COAST

Picture Acknowledgements

The Automobile Association would like to thank the following photographers, companies and picture libraries for their assistance in the preparation of this book.

Abbreviations for the picture credits are as follows: (t) top; (b) bottom; (l) left; (r) right; (AA) AA World Travel Library.

Front Cover AA/A Burton; Back Cover (main) AA/J Miller; Back Cover (inset) AA/S Anderson; 3 AA/C Warren; 5 AA/D Forss; 7 AA/C Lees; 8 AA/A Burton; 9 AA/M Busselle; 10 AA; 11 AA/J Mottershaw; 12 AA/J Wyand; 13 AA/H Williams; 14 AA; 15 AA/C Jones; 16 AA/R Moss; 17 AA; 18 AA/T Mackie; 19 AA/S McBride; 20 AA/R Ireland; 21 AA/S Whitehorne; 22 AA/M Kipling; 23 AA/C Warren; 24 AA/N Hicks; 25 AA/M Moody; 26 AA/J Miller; 27 AA/J Miller; 28 AA/R Moss; 29 AA/R Moss; 30 AA/E Ellington; 31 AA/C Warren; 32 AA/N Hicks; 33 AA/M Jourdan; 34 AA/J Miller; 35 AA/R Tenison; 36 AA/J Miller; 37 AA/N Hicks; 38 AA/J Miller; 39 AA/J Miller; 40 AA/A Burton; 41 AA/R Coulam; 42 AA/M Moody; 43 AA/N Hicks; 44 AA/A Burton; 45 AA/A Burton; 46 AA/N Hicks; 47 AA/A Burton; 48 AA/J Miller; 49 AA/N Hicks; 50 AA/J Miller; 51 AA/C Jones; 52 AA/J Miller; 53 AA/N Hicks; 54 AA/J Miller; 55 A/R Coulam; 56 AA/J Smith; 57 AA/C Jones; 58 AA/C Warren; 59 AA/R Coulam; 60 AA/R Moss; 61 AA/C Warren; 62 AA/N Hicks; 63 AA/C Warren; 64 AA/C Jones; 65 AA/S Whitehorne; 66 AA/C Jones; 67 AA/C Jones; 68 AA/C Warren; 69 AA/C Warren; 70 AA/C Warren; 71 AA/C Warren; 72 A/T Mackie; 73 AA/C Jones; 74 AA/N Jenkins; 75 AA/N Hicks; 76 AA/A Burton; 77 AA/C Jones; 78 AA/A Burton; 79 AA/T Mackie; 80 AA/A Burton; 81 AA/J Miller; 82 AA/N Hicks; 83 AA/J Miller; 84 AA/J Miller; 85 AA/J Miller; 86 AA/A Burton; 87 AA/A Burton 88 AA/T Mackie; 89 AA/S Anderson; 90 AA/M Moody; 91 AA/C Warren; 92 AA/C Warren; 93 AA/S Watkins; 94 AA/J Miller; 95 AA/C Warren

Every effort has been made to trace the copyright holders, and we apologise in advance for any accidental errors. We would be happy to apply any corrections in the following edition of this publication.

Opposite: Sunset over Compton Bay, one of the Isle of Wight's superb beaches, which is also popular with surfers.

INTRODUCTION

Spectacular coastal scenery, genteel seaside resorts, ancient harbours and ports, picturesque fishing villages and superb wildlife, Britain's 6,000-mile (9,655km) coastline incorporates cliff, headland, dune and marsh and superlatives can be used to describe every inch of it.

Head to the Lizard on the Cornish coast for far-reaching views, craggy cliffs and breezy windswept downs or the serpentine cliffs at Kynance Cove where the sea spouts and hisses. Swap these tourist honeypots for Hartland Quay in Devon and the rugged coastline and treacherous seas give a tremendous sense of space and remoteness. While Lulworth Cove, on the Purbeck Heritage Coast, is part of an astounding coastline with numerous geological phenomena, including a natural arch, a fossil forest and an incredibly rich wildlife.

An antidote to the heady heights of the cliffs are the idyllic creeks and estuaries of the South Hams in Devon, the subtropical backwaters of Helford River and the deep wooded combs of Somerset that link the uplands with sea. Head east to the flat and muddy Essex coast and the sea has reached so far inland to make a lonely wilderness of the creeks and marshes, beloved of yachtsmen and wild flowers. The estuaries of the Deben and the Orwell are reminiscent of Essex, but along the coast of north Suffolk the tides are eating away at the cliffs, part of the natural realignment of the coastline, which has already seen most of Dunwich disappear beneath the waves.

Further north, a chain golden beaches stretches up the long, smooth flank of Northumberland and along the northwest Lancashire coast as the huge sands of Dunstanburgh and Morecambe Bay glimmer under a colossal sky.

Head along Scotland's western coast and the lochs ripple sweetly below the mountains as the sun sets beyond the Western Isles. Turn to the eastern seaboard and discover dark sandy beaches, dramatic cliffs and pretty fishing villages, such as Anstruther and Crail. Reach the wilds of Wester Ross and the sea runs in among magnificent mountain scenery.

For many people, however, the archetypal coastal scene is the classic British seaside resort, perhaps the refined Victorian atmosphere of Scarborough or the bright lights of Blackpool or the limestone cliffs and sandy beaches of the Gower Peninsula. Weymouth, Cromer or Southwold, everyone has a favourite. But perhaps, in Sussex are the best-loved seaside towns – packed with history and architectural beauty, resorts such as vibrant Brighton, classy Eastbourne, family-friendly Bexhill and quirky West Wittering.

Away from the amusement arcades, the coastline supports a stunning variety and richness of both habitats and wildlife. Many of Britain's best sites for birding are also on the coast, including the Farne Islands, Northumberland, and the RSPB reserves at Minsmere in Suffolk, Titchwell in Norfolk and Leighton Moss in Lancashire. In Wales, the rugged cliffs of the Pembrokeshire Coast National Park are famous for their colonies of gannets and Manx shearwaters, while on the Solway coast, the Caerlaverock salt marshes play host to more than 12,000 barnacle geese each winter.

Each shoreline has its wildlife to discover, and coastal paths to conduct landscape lovers closer to the views they crave. On the way is an engaging parade of ports, cliff-top castles, piers, lighthouses and fishing villages.

Opposite: A small boat run aground along the Northumberland shore, with Holy Island and the castle across the water beyond.

Groynes along the 47-mile (75km) East Sussex coast prevent the sand and shingle from shifting with the prevailing southwesterly winds.
Opposite: Clinging to the end of Hengistbury Head's windswept peninsula, Mudeford's sand dunes and brightly coloured beach huts at first light.

Skomer and Skokholm, off the western tip of the Pembrokeshire mainland are — together with the more remote Grassholm Island, an RSPB reserve and the site of the largest gannetry in England and Wales — one of Europe's foremost breeding sites for sea birds. Porpoises and dolphins are also regular visitors.

Scarborough has a rich maritime history; Henry III granted a charter to build a port here in 1251, but ships have used its natural harbour since the 4th century when the Romans built a signal station here – part of an early warning system against sea raiders.

Summerleze in Bude, where the sea rolls into the shore in long, unbroken waves and the sweep of sand makes it a popular with families.
Opposite: Nash Lighthouse on the Gower Peninsula, was built in 1832 following the tragic shipwreck of a passenger steamer in 1830.

The caves, rabbit warrens and captivating scenery of Great Orme, Llandudno, bring hordes of visitors each summer, but its marine grasslands are also a Site of Special Scientific Interest (SSSI), and limestone-loving plants, such as wild thyme and bloody cranesbill thrives here.

At one time, Clovelly was famous for being the place where donkeys were used to carry goods and people from the quay up the perilously steep cobbled village street, but it is still an extraordinary place and best seen early in the morning before the arrival of hordes of tourists.

The towering cliffs at Land's End that run southeast to Gwennap Head, where they turn eastwards in a succession of surf-tossed coves and commanding headland, echoing to the rumble of the sea and the cries of gulls.

The unusual geometrically shaped sedimentary rocks of Nash Point lies on the Glamorgan Heritage Coast, a 14-mile (22.5km) stretch of coastline between Ogmore and Gileston, characterised by sandy beaches and punctuated by weathered strips of rock.

Legend tells that St Edmund was shipwrecked on the cliffs of Old Hunstanton in AD 855 and was so grateful for being spared a watery death in the Wash that he built a chapel in thanksgiving. The 13th-century ruins still stand today, looking out across the grey stormy seas.

At the extreme western tip of the Isle of Wight lies a famous British landmark – the Needles. The best viewpoint of these spectacular chalk stacks is from the Needles Old Battery, built in 1682 to defend against an attack from the French.

The Old Man of Hoy, in the remote Orkney Islands, is a 449-foot (137m) sea stack of red sandstone popular with climbers.
Opposite: The natural limestone arch of Durdle Door on the Purbeck Heritage Coast, above the long, clean, pebbly beach.

Pink heather growing along the curving expanse of Robin Hood's Bay with its infamous history of smuggling and pirates. In the distance, the small fishing village of Ravenscar, menaced by the eroding sea, clings to the edge of a steep ravine.

Sturdy Welsh Mountain ponies have grazed for centuries in the Pembrokeshire National Park.
In the distance, a view over the Ramsay Sound to Maen Bachau near peaceful St Justinians.

Dusk along the south Devon coast at Start Point to Start Point Lighthouse.

Rhossili on the southern coast on the Gower Peninsula is spectacular, and boasts dunebacked beaches of surf-swept, clean sand and magnificent limestone cliffs, chiselled in places into deep gullies and knife-edge ridges.

A seagull over the sea at Eastbourne – the cries of wheeling gulls is probably one of the most enduring sounds and images of the British seaside.

West Wittering's superb beach, tucked away on a peninsula at the mouth of Chichester Harbour. Before this stretch of coast became fashionable with visitors, the open fields extended to the beach, providing a natural playground for children.

The setting sun over the rocky, serpentine coastal headland of Kynance Cove, west of Lizard Point.

Opposite: The fortress-like Lizard Lighthouse built in 1751 dominates the Cornish coast to the east.

Overlooking the Bay of Skaill in Orkney, the coast-side settlement at Skara Brae dates from 3100 BC. The houses and connecting passageways that formed the ancient farming settlement are remarkably well preserved.

Whitesands, part of the superb 230-mile (370km) Pembrokeshire Coast National Park, which is followed, for most of the way, by the Pembrokeshire Coast Path – a wonderful rollercoaster walk with secluded sandy bays, rugged cliffs and ever-changing seascapes.

The seaside holiday is a relatively modern invention. Until the 18th century, the sea was generally distrusted as a dangerous and disagreeable element and the change of attitude stemmed more from concern with health than with fun.

A Punch & Judy tent on Weymouth beach advertises the time of the next show. The caricature puppets have their roots in 16th-century Italian commedia dell'arte, but this traditional beach-side entertainment remains as popular with children (and adults) today.

In the Middle Ages, Hastings was an important harbour and fishing is still a major industry here. The town has the largest beach-launched fishing fleet in Europe and the 'Deeles', tall wooden huts used for storing fishing nets, are unique to the town.

Surfing reigns supreme in North Cornwall on a series of superb beaches between Bude and Newquay. Watergate Bay (above) has some of the best waves that Cornwall has to offer while Fistral Beach is an international surfing venue.

Torquay is south Devon at its most Mediterranean with its balmy climate, palm trees and million-pound yachts basking in the marina.
Opposite: A traditional, colourful carousel on the seafront at Brighton complements the many attractions found on the pier.

A row of beach huts at low tide at Bexhill, a quiet late-Victorian and Edwardian seaside town on the East Sussex coast, which became the first mixed bathing beach in Britain in 1901.

Brighton's elegant beachfront juxtaposes traditional striped deckchairs, elegant Victorian lamp posts, aqua-coloured railings and bow-windowed Regency and Victorian façades with the brash and noisy atmosphere at Brighton Pier with its funfair and white-knuckle rides.

Sunrise over Studland, Dorset. Behind the superb, dunebacked beach, which sports sun-loving naturists in warm weather, lies the old rugged heath, now an important nature reserve in the care of English Nature and the National Trust.

Opposite: The Farne Islands is home to a large population of characterful puffins – called Tommy Noddies locally, due to their bobbing-style gait.

The ancestor of the seaside resort was the spa and towns, such as Scarborough, offered a combination of smart socialising and health-giving mineral waters, but by 1753 visitors were nervously entering the sea itself and the fad for bathing moved to Brighton and the seaside resort was born.

A stunning view from Appledore across the mouth of the River Torridge to Saunton Sands with colourful sailing craft dotting the sands at low tide – a typical picturesque and peaceful coastal scene in Devon.

Dusk sets over Swanage, with the charismatic jetty in the foreground and the headland of Studland Bay behind. Swanage is famous for its elegant buildings and its Victorian pier, which has recently been beautifully restored. People are invited to assist in the pier's upkeep by sponsoring a plank. In return, the sponsor has their name inscribed on a brass plaque, which is attached to one of the planks on the pier.

The sun sets over the peaceful promenade at Boscombe beach, Bournemouth – the queen of the south coast holiday resorts – her 6 miles (9.6km) of golden sands stretch from the ancient settlement at Hengistbury Head to the white sands and millionnaire's mansions of Canford Cliffs.

The familiar seaside sight of a seagull, here sitting atop a retro-style beach cafe in Paignton, Devon.

Seaweed-covered groynes leading up to the beach huts in Calshot. This long stretch of shoreline backed by pines is known for its valuable habitats – shingle beaches, reed beds, marsh and brackish ponds – which attract marine and birdlife.

The extraordinary stretch of coast at Fairlight, East Sussex, which supports a great variety of wildlife – peregrines, fulmars and black redstarts may be glimpsed on the sandstone cliffs and bottlenose dolphins and harbour porpoises offshore.

A beautiful, wooded combe leads down to the pebble beach at Heddon Mouth, a rocky cove on the coast of West Exmoor.

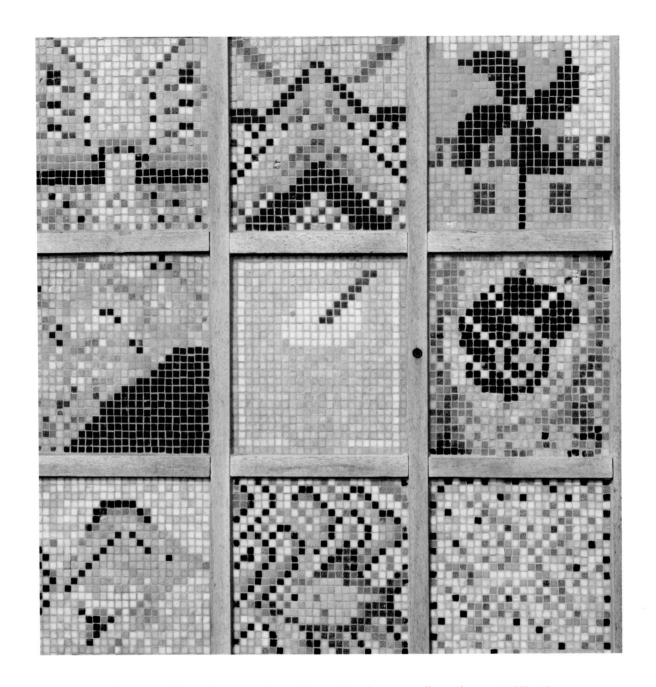

Detail of a colourful mosaic on a seafront shelter at Shoreham, a small seaside resort in West Sussex.
Opposite: Dusk falls over Lancashire's champion seaside resort, Blackpool, with its Central Pier, Ferris Wheel and Tower.

A surfer enjoying the superb waves at Saunton Sands in Devon.
Opposite: Sheltered by the South Downs, the blue and yellow beach huts at Littlehampton in West Sussex.

The elegant seafront at Eastbourne with its ornate Victorian pier, designed by Eugenius Birch and completed in 1872, has fairy-lights strung between lamp-posts and some of the best surviving ironwork and kisoks of the era.

The picturesque coastal village of Alnmouth, in Northumberland, was established in 1150 and became an important grain and shipbuilding port by the 13th century. Today, Alnmouth's superb sandy beach attracts holidaymakers and walkers.

The atmospheric and sea-battered ruins of St Andrews Castle in Fife, overlooking the small Castle Sands beach.
Built on this rocky promontory for the Archbishops of St Andrews, the castle dates from the 13th century.

One of Cornwall's most romantic images – the view of the castellated St Michael's Mount from the shore of Marazion at high tide. At low tide the approach is on foot along a fine, cobbled causeway.

St Govan's Chapel on the Pembrokeshire Coast, a 12th-century stone building tucked away in a deep cleft in the cliffs, west of St Govan's Head. The cliffs form part of a unique habitat, which supports breeding chough pairs and nest sites for guillemots, razorbills and peregrines.

The romantic ruin of Dunstanburgh Castle on the beautiful Northumberland coast. The castle was originally built to protect a small harbour, which was surrounded on three sides by the sea and a moat on its fourth.

Three miles (4.8km) of windswept dunes of golden sand provides a dramatic backdrop to Hayle's superb, sandy beach that is popular with sand yachts and kite-buggy enthusiasts.

Located 2 miles (3.2km) west of St Davids and in the Pembrokeshire Coast National Park, the wildlife-rich and beautiful Whitesands Bay is backed by sand dunes and, on a clear day, has superb views of St David's Head and Ramsay Island.

Limpets clinging onto the rocks at Heddon's Mouth, Exmoor National Park.

Seaweed on Marloes beach, Pembrokeshire Coast National Park, which is known for its remote and wild landscape, unusual rock formations and views of Skokholm Island – founded in the 17th century, it was the first bird reserve in Britain.

A view to Mumbles Head Lighthouse, where the wild and rugged Gower coast collides with the more urban, seaside attractions of Swansea.

Ringed by steep wooded slopes and with stunning views across to the neighbouring islands of Coll and Tiree, Calgary Bay, on the Isle of Mull, is one of Scotland's most beautiful beaches.

The coastal landscape of the Valley of Rocks just west of Lynton is extraordinary; the craggy dry valley is unique on Exmoor, and characterised by jagged sandstone tors, formed as a result of weathering processes over thousands of years.

Devon's northwest tip is characterised by an extraordinary change in the nature of the coast, from calm, flat-topped cliffs to the harsh, rocky coastline of Hartland Quay – its history peppered with tales of shipwrecks and smuggling.

A superb view over the rocky coastline at Trevellan, near Bosherston in the Pembrokeshire National Park, which is popular with climbers.

The spectacular beach of Marloes Sands, in the Pembrokeshire Coast National Park, is cared for the National Trust and has fantastic opportunities for birding, while the rock pools and seaweed-strewn rocks at low tide keep children of all ages amused.

The small tidal inlet of Porth Clais in St David's Peninsula is a Site of Special Scientific Interest (SSSI) for its maritime vegetation, important habitats for invertebrates and breeding birds, such as rock pipits and oyster catchers.

The Pembrokeshire Coast Path leads down onto Whitesands Bay with distant views of Ramsay Island, home to the largest colony of grey seals in southwest Britain.

"You should have gone to Cromer, my dear," advised Mr Woodhouse in Jane Austen's Emma. *Cromer is still a refined and popular resort and Cromer crabs are prized by seafood chefs and gourmets for their tender white flesh.*

Famously depicted in John Fowles' novel, The French Lieutenant's Woman, *and Jane Austen's* Sense and Sensibility, *the Cobb at Lyme Regis was constructed in the 13th century to protect the town from the sea. The sheltered harbour is Dorset's second largest port and an active fishing port.*

The pride of the Gower Peninsula is the sea-scraped Rhossili Beach towards Worms Head – a perfect, gently arcing sandy beach flanked by 250-foot (76m) sandstone cliffs and the steep grassy flanks of Rhossili Down.

A bird's footprint in the sand at Saunton Sands – one of the best beaches in Devon, a 3-mile (4.8km)
curve of golden sands backed by grassy dunes, which is popular with surfers and families.

Bournemouth beach at sunrise. The huge beaches, attractive resort and the town's proximity to the New Forest National Park and the Purbeck Heritage Coast makes Bournemouth a popular destination for holiday-makers and weekend visitors.

Sunset over the tip of the Lizard Peninsula, Britain's most southerly point. Along the coast,
the cliffs rise to 200 feet (60m) and are broken by little rocky coves.

Sunrise over Calshot, one of the settlements in the New Forest National Park and famous for its castle built by Henry VIII.
Opposite: The sun sinks below the horizon at Burnham Overy Staithe on the beautiful Norfolk coast.

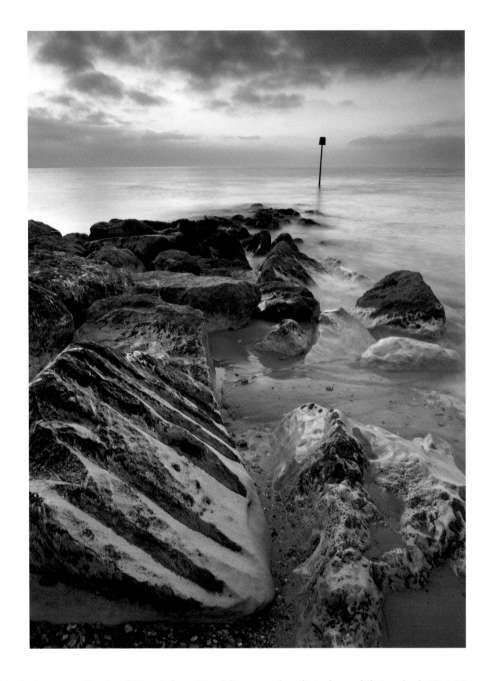

The windswept peninsula of Hengistbury Head has an archaeological record dating back 12,500 years, when Stone-Age hunter-gatherers left the remains of a camp site on its outer, seaward edge.

A rollercoaster of turf-capped white cliffs undulates between Seaford and Eastbourne rising to seven mini-peaks,
known as the Seven Sisters − a spectacular reminder that Britain was once joined to France.

Across Porlock Bay, Exmoor National Park, from the old coastguard viewpoint on Hurlstone Point. During the 18th century, as a measure against smuggling, coastguards walked the coast path all night and in all weathers, one man for every 0.25 mile (400m).

Windswept tree above the Seven Sisters at Crowlink — with Seaford Head to the west and Beachy Head to the east — this area makes up the longest and most scenic stretch of undeveloped coast in Britain.

The high chalk ridge of the South Downs ends at the south coast in spectacular style
with a range of dazzling white cliffs at Beachy Head and the Seven Sisters.

A world-renowned example of Modernist architecture, the De la Warr Pavilion, is the rather surprising seafront centrepiece of the quiet late-Victorian and Edwardian seaside town of Bexhill in East Sussex.

A chalk stack off the coast at Freshwater Bay in the Isle of Wight. The area is famous for being the home of Alfred, Lord Tennyson, and the inspiration for many of his best-loved poems.

Sunset at Kimmeridge Bay, looking towards Clavel Tower on the headland of the Jurassic Coast in Dorset.

The evening light casts a warm glow on the buildings and waters of picturesque Oban Bay in Argyll and Bute.

Opposite: Boats moored at Burnham Overy Staithe in Norfolk. Horatio Nelson was born nearby at Burnham Thorpe in 1758.

The wild and unspoilt Caldey Island, located 3 miles (4.8km) off the south Pembrokeshire coastline, near Tenby, is home to a large population of grey seals. Half of the world's population of grey seals are found on and around British coasts.

The Marloes Peninsula forms the westernmost tip of the southern shores of St Brides Bay on the Pembrokeshire Coast.
Famous for its stunning scenery and wonderfully rugged coastline, the secluded coves are also often inhabited by seals.

A misty dawn breaks at Lawrenny, Pembrokeshire, with its picturesque yachting station and attractive quayside.
Near by, walkers can enjoy wandering through the oldest native oak woodlands in Britain.

South Stack lighthouse on Holy Island, Anglesey, is still a fully operational lighthouse. The lighthouse can be visited and the island is reached by descending 160 steps down to a suspension bridge.

An iconic symbol of the British seaside, Brighton Pier has been a place of entertainment for more than a century.
Opposite: Skomer and Skokholm, famous for their puffins, rare Manx shearwaters, colonies of guillemots, razorbills and storm petrels.

INDEX